BE A BETTER
Real Estate
AGENT

I0078409

REAL ESTATE MARKETING MAGIC

The Art of Visibility and Value

Mini Mastery *Series*

Donna Wysinger

Copyright 2025 © Be a Better Agent

Copyright Notice

Real Estate Marketing Magic:
The Art of Visibility and Value
Copyright © 2025 by Be a Better Agent
All rights reserved.

No part of this book may be reproduced, stored in a retrieval system, or transmitted in any form or by any means; electronic, mechanical, photocopying, recording, or otherwise, without prior written permission from the author, except for brief quotations used in a review.

This book is intended for informational and personal use only. The author and publisher are not responsible for any actions or outcomes resulting from the use of the content within. The exercises and prompts are meant to inspire creativity and positive business practices and should not replace professional advice when needed.

ISBN: 979-8-9930660-2-8

Be a Better Agent

For permissions, inquiries, or further information, please email:
Donna@BeABetterAgent.com

Dedication

To the trailblazers, marketers-with-heart, and mentors who showed me that real estate isn't just about selling homes, it's about sharing your light and serving with soul ...

Thank you for modeling what it means to lead with purpose, show up with integrity, and make marketing meaningful. Your example lit the way for this book to be written.

To the clients, colleagues, family, and friends who've cheered me on, trusted me with your homes, and shared my name generously ...

Your support has been the magic behind my momentum. Every referral, kind word, and opportunity to serve has helped me shape a business rooted in connection, care, and visibility that feels aligned.

This book is a tribute to all of you, and the marketing magic we create together.

Thank you.

TABLE OF CONTENTS

TABLE OF CONTENTS

- Dream Client Avatar
- Branding Checklist
- SOI Connections Schedule
- Seller and Buyer Lead Follow Up Campaigns
- Social Media Prompts for Creating Posts
- Nourishing Practices for the Magnetic You

Foreword

If you've ever felt like marketing wasn't your thing or worried that putting yourself out there meant being pushy or fake, I'm here to remind you: marketing is simply allowing yourself to be seen. When you lead with heart, values, and genuine care, marketing becomes a natural extension of who you are, not something you have to force or fake.

This guide was created to help you find your flow. It is about visibility that feels aligned, joyful, and authentic. It is also about helping the right people discover you, not by shouting, but by shining. You don't need to be the loudest in the room. You just need to show up in a way that feels true to you.

Inside these pages, you'll find strategies that are doable, sustainable, and heartfelt, infused with creativity, generosity, and a bit of sparkle. Whether you're working to build your brand, grow your reach, or stay visible without burnout, my hope is that this guide feels like a trusted companion on your journey.

You are worthy of being seen. Your work matters. And your people are looking for you.

Let's help them find you ...
with a little marketing magic.

Donna Wysinger
Owner/Founder
Be a Better Agent

INTRODUCTION

Where the REAL MARKETING Begins

Let's begin with something that's been misunderstood for far too long:

Marketing yourself isn't selfish, it's essential.

… In fact, it's one of the most generous things you can do.

Visibility isn't vanity. It's value made visible.

Because when you show up, speak clearly, and let the world know who you are and how you serve, you're not "self-promoting." **You're making it easier for the people who need you to find you.**

As agents, we often fall into the trap of thinking: *"If I just do great work, people will come."* Or, *"If I post once or twice and update my headshot, that should be enough."*

But the truth?

We live in a loud, fast-moving world. People aren't going to magically stumble across your brilliance. They need to be **shown the way**. And more importantly, they need to understand the value you bring.

Marketing is how we bridge that gap.

It's how we stay visible, build trust, and help people remember us when it matters most.

📖 What This Book Is – and What It's Not

This is not a guide about hard sell tactics, complex funnels, or cookie-cutter methods. It's not about becoming someone you're not. It's not about being everywhere, all the time, with zero boundaries.

Instead, this is a guide about **authentic marketing** that feels good. It's about showing up as yourself, being proud of the work you do, and allowing your personality, passion, and presence to be part of your brand.

It's about crafting a message that feels *real*, not rehearsed. It's about aligning your visibility with your values. It's about helping people see your value before you ever walk through their front door.

And yes...
it's about a little bit
of marketing magic.

Learning to Be Seen and Valued 😎

When I first started in real estate, most of the sales courses I attended were all about cold calls, and door knocking, and buying leads. I learned scripts to use on friends and family and even strangers. I felt like a big part of my job was to badger everyone around me until they would either promise to use me or send me to someone who might. I felt stressed and anxious all of the time.

I decided very quickly that real estate was *"maybe money,"* so I kept my day job and worked hard at both careers. Occasionally I helped someone with buying or selling, and I hoped success would follow.

I wasn't sharing my voice, or my experience, or my passion for serving. I wasn't allowing people to see me as a real estate specialist, even when I got pretty good at it. Everyone always knew me as my *"other job."*

It wasn't until I started embracing my own story, my unique way of connecting with clients, my care-driven approach, my creative side, my real talk, that **everything shifted.**

People began reaching out, not because I had flashy ads or the perfect social media strategy. Instead, it was because I was *visible*. Because I was me.

I built a brand around that **visibility**. Around **authenticity**. Around **value**.

And now, **I would love to help you do the same.**

Whether you're new to real estate or decades in ...

Whether you've got a marketing plan or a pile of *"I'll get to it someday"* ideas ...

Whether you love putting yourself out there or it makes you a little *(or a lot)* uncomfortable ...

This guide is here to help you shine brighter, show up smarter, and be seen for the incredible agent you already are.

Because you don't have to be loud to be powerful.

You don't have to be flashy to be magnetic.

**You simply have to be visible ...
and you need to be YOU!**

You already have the skills. You already have the heart *(or you wouldn't be reading this book)*. Now it's time to make sure your clients, future referrals, friends, family, everyone you know can see it.

Let's make your message magnetic.

Let's help your marketing feel like YOU.

Let's work a little Real Estate Marketing Magic ... together.

CHAPTER 1

Know Your WHO

If you've ever been told, *"You need to farm a neighborhood,"* or *"Pick a zip code and start mailing,"* then you've probably felt the pull of old-school advice that focuses on location or demographics over connection.

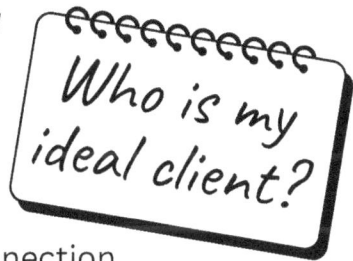

Who is my ideal client?

And while knowing your service area is important, what is **much more powerful is knowing your people.**

When you are using **relationship-centered marketing,** which is the heartbeat of this guide, your clients don't come to you just because of where you work or where you live. **They come to you because of who you are and how you help.** They have a sense that you're the one who will take care of them and understand them.

In this chapter, we're going to go deeper than postcodes and postcards. We're going to help you define and attract your dream clients and ideal referral connections, the ones who energize you, align with your values, and help your business grow with ease and joy.

Define Your Dream Clients and Referral Partners

Let's start with your ideal home seller or homebuyer.

These are the ones who make your work feel fun, fulfilling, and deeply aligned. They're the folks you'd happily help move again *(and again)* because working with them felt natural. They got you. They trusted you. They respected the process.

Take a moment to reflect:

- What qualities do your dream clients share?
- What stage of life are they in?
- What are they looking for beyond a house?
- What do they care about most in a real estate transaction?

And just as important:

Who are your favorite connection partners?

- The local lender who makes the process smooth?
- The hairstylist who knows everyone in town?
- The past client who tags you in every Facebook group thread asking for a *"good Realtor"*?

Write these people down. Notice the patterns. You're not just building a list — you're building a **client compass**.

_____   _____
_____   _____
_____   _____
_____   _____
_____   _____
_____   _____
_____   _____
_____   _____
_____   _____
_____   _____
_____   _____

💎 Understand What Makes You Uniquely Valuable

You are not like every other agent. And you shouldn't try to be. You have strengths, skills, and life experiences that position you to serve your audience in ways others can't.

Pause and consider:

- What do people say they love about working with you?
- What do you wish more people knew about your process or your values?
- What personal stories or life experiences help you connect more deeply?

Your "who" becomes clearer when you match their needs with your strengths.

You're not just a real estate agent, you're a **trusted guide, advocate,** and **connector**. Own that.

Niche Without Fear: How Focusing Brings Freedom 🖱️

Let's bust a myth: **Niching doesn't limit you, it launches you.** When you narrow your focus, you make it easier for the right people to say,

"She's exactly who I need."

Trying to speak to everyone waters down your message. But speaking directly to your people? That builds instant trust.

Whether your niche is:

- First-time homebuyers
- LGBTQ+ seniors looking for inclusive communities
- Busy families relocating across states
- Divorcees selling and starting over
- Veterans using VA loans to purchase

... You don't have to *exclude* others to focus on the ones you best serve. In fact, you'll find over time that referrals from your dream clients will expand *beyond* your niche once people understand who you are and how well you take care of others.

🧭 Create a "Client Compass" to Guide Your Marketing

Now that you know who you're speaking to, let's build a compass you can return to every time you create content, plan events, or connect with your community.

Your **Client Compass** is like a customer avatar. It should include:

- **WHO:** Describe your dream client and top referrers.
- **WHAT:** What challenges do they have that you solve?
- **WHY YOU:** Why do they love working with you? What value do you bring?
- **HOW:** What's your tone, vibe, and voice when you communicate?

Keep this compass nearby. Refer to it when writing a social post, planning a pop-by, or prepping a listing consultation.

Because when your marketing speaks directly to your *"who,"* it becomes effortless, magnetic, and meaningful.

Ready to start attracting them? In the next chapter, we'll show you how to build a relationships-focused funnel that naturally brings your dream clients to your door, and keeps them coming back.

Let's keep the magic moving!

🔑 Key Reflections

Who are the clients I feel most energized and aligned working with and what do they all have in common?

_____

_____

_____

_____

_____

What unique strengths, experiences, or qualities do I have that make me the right agent for my dream clients?

_____

_____

_____

_____

_____

_____

How can I start refining my marketing message to speak more directly to the people I genuinely want to attract?

_____

_____

_____

_____

_____

NOTES

DOODLES

CHAPTER 2

Build a BRAND
They'll REMEMBER

Clarity in your message creates connection in your business.

If visibility is how people see you, then messaging is what they remember about you. Your message is the golden thread that runs through everything you do; your website, your social posts, your emails, even the way you introduce yourself at a community event. It's how people understand who you are, what you do, and most importantly, why they should choose *you*.

Crafting a business message involves creating a **clear, concise, and compelling narrative that resonates with your target audience** and effectively communicates your brand's unique value. It connects with customers on an emotional level, builds trust, and motivates them to take action.

⚡ Marketing Begins with YOU

Every standout brand begins with a simple truth: people don't buy houses from logos, taglines, or clever slogans.

They choose you; your energy, your vibe, your voice. And yet, when it's time to "market ourselves," so many agents freeze. We second guess, overthink, and try to mimic someone else's message because it looks polished, catchy, or *"professional."*

However, the most magnetic marketing doesn't come from trying to sound slick, it comes from speaking your truth with clarity and connection.

We want to help you discover and craft your message so it reflects the **real you**, resonates with the **right people**, and feels good every time you share it.

Write a Marketing Message That Reflects Who You Are 💬

Gone are the days of templated bios and robotic pitches. Your clients want to work with a human, someone who is relatable, trustworthy, and real. Start by considering:

- What do I believe about real estate and service?
- What's unique about how I guide clients through the buying or selling process?
- What qualities do others appreciate about working with me?

This is not about bragging. It's about anchoring into your truth — and letting it shine in your message.

꒐꒐꒐꒐꒐ Identify What Your Audience Needs to Hear
Not Just What You Offer

While it's tempting to list credentials or services, what your audience really needs is reassurance. They want to know:

- Can I trust you?
- Will you care about me and my needs?
- Will you make this easier for me?

When you determine how best to serve your clients, consider what kinds of emotions they might be experiencing when they talk with you. What kinds of questions keep them awake at night? What can *you* do to bring them relief, trust… and peace?

Craft your message around those needs. Instead of saying, *"I've been in real estate for 20 years,"* you might say, *"I help people feel calm and confident in every step of their real estate journey."* Let your message reflect what they want to *feel*, not just what you do.

Create a Tagline That Sets You Apart

A powerful one-liner or tagline isn't created to be cute *(although it can be),* it anchors your brand and gives people something to remember and repeat.

To create yours, use this simple framework:

I help [who] do/achieve [what], without [pain point], so they can [desired result].

Examples:

- *"I help growing families upsize with ease, so they can stop tripping over toys and start loving their space."*
- *"Selling with me means more peace, more joy, and more in your pocket."*
- *"I help first-time homebuyers buy with clarity (not confusion), so they can move in with confidence."*
- *"We help homeowners sell with confidence and clarity, without overwhelm, so they can move forward with peace and prosperity."*

Or go short and bold:

- *"Helping you find your place of peace."*
- *"Where calm meets closing."*
- *"Where feel-good moves meet top-dollar results."*
- *"I turn 'just listed' into 'just celebrated.'"*
- *"Real estate with soul, style, and spirit"* (this is the one I use)

Align Your Voice Across All of Your Marketing

Once you've defined your message, let it show up everywhere. Make sure your website bio, email signature, social media, business card, items of value, and even your voicemail reflect the same energy and promise.

Consistency builds trust. When your voice is aligned, your brand becomes magnetic.

The goal is **consistency with warmth**. Your audience should feel like they *"know"* you no matter where they meet you.

PRO TIP

Use your new message as your marketing filter. If a piece of content doesn't feel like it aligns with your message and mission, skip it or tweak it.

Message First, Marketing Second

Your brand message is your beacon. It tells people who you are, what you believe, and how you help.

When your message is clear, everything else becomes easier; your social media posts, your website content, your listing presentation, your buyer consultation. All of your interactions with the people you care about and help.

Because you're no longer trying to sell, you're just showing up as you.

Your message is your magic.

When your words truly reflect your heart, you don't need flashy gimmicks or pushy tactics. Your authenticity does the heavy lifting. People feel it. They connect with it. They remember it. That's the real power of a message crafted with care. It builds trust before the conversation even begins.

🔑 Key Reflections

What words or phrases do people often use to describe me when referring me to others? *(These may be clues to my most natural and magnetic message.)*

_____

_____

_____

_____

If my dream client is reading my website or bio, what do I want them to *feel?* And what do I want them to know about me right away?

_____

_____

_____

_____

_____

_____

What tagline or *"mini message"* captures the heart of my business in one clear, meaningful sentence?

_____

_____

_____

_____

_____

NOTES

DOODLES

CHAPTER 3

ENGAGE and GROW
Your REFERRAL Base

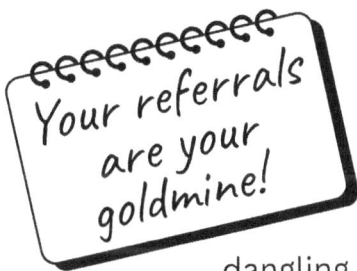

Your referrals are your goldmine!

I want to make this part very clear: this is not the kind of funnel you see in so many online marketing masterclasses. You won't be luring strangers with clickbait or dangling free PDFs in exchange for email addresses you'll never use.

You are a real estate professional building a real business with real humans. This means your funnel is going to feel just like you; warm, honest, helpful, and caring.

In a relationship-based business, your funnel isn't about transactions. It's about transformation. It's the gentle, intentional journey someone takes from first noticing you, to genuinely trusting you, to joyfully hiring you, and then telling their friends to do the same.

⏬ Referrals Are Already in the Funnel

Most people think of a *"sales funnel"* as a straight line: awareness → interest → decision → action. But when it comes to referrals, your funnel isn't linear. It's more like a spiral staircase that keeps looping people closer in, over time.

Referrals start halfway down the funnel. That's the magic. A warm referral skips over the hardest part: building initial awareness and trust. Instead, your happy client, best friend, neighbor, or vendor has already paved the way with credibility and connection.

So, while others are spending thousands on SEO and ads just to maybe be seen, your name is already being passed hand-to-hand, **with a glowing recommendation attached.**

That's why nurturing your referral funnel is pure gold. It's the most soul-aligned, cost-effective, joy-filled path to consistent business.

Map the Journey 📍

Even though your clients may find you through referral, they still travel a path with you. And when you understand that journey, you can show up with intention at each stage.

Here's a simple way to look at it:

- **Awareness** – They've heard your name, seen a post, met you briefly, or received your pop-by.
- **Trust** – They've read your reviews, followed you online, chatted with their referrer, or seen you at a community event.
- **Connection** – You've had a conversation, shared resources, or made them feel seen.
- **Decision** – They've hired you or passed your name along to someone else!

You don't have to do *everything* at every stage. You just need to stay visible and valuable in ways that feel natural to you. This is where your marketing starts to feel more like service, and less like shouting into the void.

👆 Build Touchpoints That Feel Like You

Pop-bys, social media, personal notes, community events, email newsletters, workshops, open houses, housewarming gifts, vendor spotlights... these are all beautiful ways to show up for your people.

Each one is a *"Hello Again"* on their journey. Each one reminds them of your message:

I am here. I care. I can help.

And when you approach these touchpoints with heart *(not hustle)*, people feel it. You're not just staying *"top of mind,"* you're staying close to their hearts.

Ask yourself:

- Where do my people naturally gather?
- Where can I show up most authentically *(online or off)*?
- What do I love doing that makes others feel seen and supported?

Those answers become the framework of your referral funnel. And over time, **as your presence ripples outward, referrals flow inward.**

Events, Pop-Bys, and Socials That Spark Connection

These three touchpoints are powerful tools in your funnel. Not because they sell something, but because they celebrate something.

Events:

From appreciation parties to educational workshops, events create shared moments. They deepen connection and offer natural opportunities to say, *"I'm here when you need me. And I'm someone you'll enjoy working with."*

Pop-Bys:

Pop-bys are small gifts delivered with big heart. These tiny, thoughtful touches say, *"You matter to me."* They're unforgettable and sharable, especially when they're clever, seasonal, or just plain fun.

Social Media:

This is where your brand voice lives day-to-day. It's where people get to know you. Not just as a real estate agent, but as a person. The one who loves dogs, or posts about her clients' big wins... and shares a little sparkle every week.

When you consistently use these tools with heart and intention, you're not building a funnel, **you're building a community.**

🛡️ You Don't Need to Be Everywhere ... Just Be Present

Let's take the pressure off. You don't have to master every platform or throw huge parties every month. But you do need to show up.

Because presence builds trust, and trust builds your referral base... and your business.

Start small.

Be consistent.

And most of all ... BE YOU!

🔑 Key Reflections

Where do I feel most natural and authentic when connecting with my audience *(online or offline)*?

_____

_____

_____

_____

_____

What are 3 recurring touchpoints I could commit to this year to stay visible and valuable?

_____

_____

_____

_____

_____

Who in my referral circle could I collaborate with to co-host an event or share pop-by deliveries?

_____

_____

_____

_____

_____

NOTES

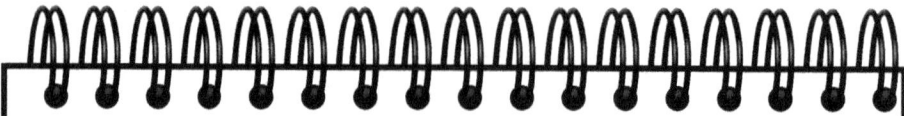

DOODLES

You DON'T Need Paid
ADS or LEADS

You do not need to be a social media ad wizard or SEO expert or spend hundreds of dollars a month buying leads to grow a successful real estate business. In fact, many of the best agents you admire likely built their brands and businesses

YOU are your brand's most powerful asset. OWN IT.

through **meaningful relationships, authentic visibility, and consistent connection** — not clicks.

And that's great news, because it means you can build your business in a way that actually feels good. You don't need to master algorithms or burn your budget on cold traffic. You simply need to focus on showing up where it matters most: in the hearts, minds, and inboxes of the people who already know, love, and trust you, and the people they send your way.

📢 When Paying for Advertising CAN Work

Let's be clear: paid advertising isn't bad. There's a time and place where it makes sense, like promoting a special event, launching a new service, or boosting an already high-performing post to get extra traction.

But too often, agents pour money into online ads without insight, confidence, or strategy. They hope that if they just throw enough dollars at the internet, new clients will magically appear. What usually happens? Crickets. Or worse, cold leads who ghost.

It's not just about whether you're visible. **It's about how you're showing up**. People don't want to be sold to. They want to connect with someone they trust.

Attraction vs. Chasing: The Real Difference 🏃🏃

Think of traditional ads like waving down strangers on a sidewalk: *"Hey! You wanna buy a house? I can help!"* *The* only way they would be at all interested in what you are saying is if they were considering buying or selling. And you haven't built any rapport with them, so the chances are fairly low that they would respond.

Now picture attraction-based marketing: you're having a great time at a barbecue, talking with people, sharing stories, laughing. And someone leans in and says, *"Hey, my sister is thinking of selling. Can I give her your number?"*

That's the power of attraction. It feels better. It *works* better. And it doesn't cost a dime.

Why SOI and Referrals Convert Better Than Cold Leads ⇄🚶🏃

Your sphere of influence *(SOI)* and their referrals aren't just contacts, they're **connectors**. These are people who already know you, like you, and trust you. When someone refers you, they're vouching for your heart, your hustle, and your results. That's a powerful foundation to build a client relationship on.

By contrast, cold leads; from online ads, lead services, or random sign-ups, don't know you from the next agent. You'll have to work many times as hard *(and usually with not a lot of return)* to gain their trust.

I'm not saying cold leads don't work. Some agents work these systems well. But over time, statistics have shown that it requires a lot more work to convert those leads to sales. And... *this* book is all about creating a marketing strategy that feels aligned, organic, and *easeful*.

🫧 Focus on Connections, Not Clicks

Instead of chasing numbers, plan to focus your time and energy on the people who already believe in you:

- Your current and past clients
- Your neighbors and community
- Your friends and family
- Your local partners and vendors

These are your SOI. Send them helpful information. Invite them to client appreciation events. Check in just because. Show up for them, and they'll show up for you.

Because when your business is built on connection, every message becomes magnetic. Every social post becomes a story. Every coffee date becomes a door of possibility.

Real Magic Doesn't Cost Money – It Pays Intention Dividends

This isn't about doing more. It's about doing what matters. It's about building trust. It's about engaging in activities that light you up. And it's about creating connections and systems that keep you in flow. Aaaand **it's about having a successful and thriving business that you are proud of**.

Marketing doesn't have to mean fancy ads or guerrilla tactics.

What it *can* mean:

- Sending a thoughtful text
- Dropping off a pop-by gift
- Sharing a behind-the-scenes moment online
- Volunteering to help at a friend's event
- Having lunch with a vendor partner

When you do these things with heart and consistency, people notice. You won't need to chase attention. You'll attract it; the good kind, the right kind, the kind that creates **client connections for life.**

🔑 Key Reflections

Where am I currently spending time, energy, or money chasing leads? How could I redirect that into building real connections instead?

_____

_____

_____

_____

_____

What has felt most natural and joyful for me when it comes to marketing? How can I do more of that?

_____

_____

_____

_____

_____

Who in my sphere already trusts me, and how can I deepen that relationship with a heart-felt, intentional touchpoint this week?

_____

_____

_____

_____

_____

NOTES

NOTES

DOODLES

CHAPTER **5**

The POWER of
PASSIVE Marketing

Visibility with integrity creates trust before the first handshake.

What if you could stay top of mind without the need to be creating and sharing and showing up ... every single day?

Welcome to the world of **passive marketing**, the art of setting up systems that work for you, even when you're focused elsewhere. Passive doesn't mean disengaged or lazy; it means intentional, strategic, and **designed for sustainability**. It's your silent partner, showing up for your brand 24/7 without constant check-ins.

Think of passive marketing as the *"background music"* of your business. You may not always notice it, but it sets the tone, creates a vibe, and makes everything more cohesive. When done well, it plays a big role in why people feel drawn to you... even before you meet.

🧠 It's Not About Doing Less – It's About Working Smarter

You only have so many hours in the day. And when you're juggling listings, showings, paperwork, and personal life, your marketing can't always be front and center. That's why **passive strategies** matter so much. They let your message echo across multiple platforms, consistently and powerfully.

From the moment someone visits your website, picks up your brochure, or receives a postcard from you, they should experience your brand's personality. These are touchpoints that tell a story. Your story. They work while you sleep, while you're at a showing, or while you're flipping burgers at that neighborhood barbecue.

Your Silent Sales Team: Print, Digital & Branded Materials 📄

Here are a few passive tools that pack a punch:

- **Your Website**: More than a business card, your site is your digital home. Is it warm, welcoming, and aligned with who you are? Include personal touches, testimonials, a blog, or a simple *"Why I Love Real Estate"* section. These elements quietly connect with people at any hour.

- **Branded Print**: Guides, items of value, mailers, newsletters, email banners, listing and buyer materials, can all help build familiarity. When your face, logo, or tagline shows up consistently in your SOI's mailbox or inbox, you build trust without saying a word.

PRO TIP Create branded images to send in a text - like mini flyers for events or a Happy Birthday meme. OR... create a quick video you can send to explain a part of the transaction process.

- **Signage**: Don't underestimate a beautifully designed yard sign or open house directional. People notice consistent, polished presentation. And it makes you memorable.

- **Branded Gifts**: Whether it's a seasonal pop-by, a thank-you bag, or a closing gift, each branded moment is a quiet reminder of your care and presence.

The Real Magic: Client Care Systems & Auto Follow-Ups ⚙️

This is where passive turns into *personal*. Having systems in place to automatically check in with clients, before, during, and after the transaction, is one of the smartest investments you can make.

- **Pre-written emails and checklists** for active buyers and sellers
- **Post-transaction surveys** or home anniversary cards
- **Quarterly check-ins** via text or newsletter
- **CRM-based reminders** for client birthdays, loan anniversaries, or neighborhood market updates

Your clients feel seen, valued, and remembered . And you don't have to reinvent the wheel every time. *(That's marketing magic.)*

You don't need a fancy system to get started, just a simple spreadsheet or calendar can help you track names, birthdays, key dates, and gift ideas. If you're a fan of tech tools, customer relationship management *(CRM)* platforms like **Top Producer, Follow Up Boss,** or **By Referral Only** offer automated reminders and email templates to keep you consistent. Even a shared Google Sheet with recurring alerts can go a long way in making sure no one slips through the cracks.

The key is to create repeatable steps that reflect your brand. Map out what you want to do for every client: When do you check in while your buyers or sellers are under contract? What happens 30 days after closing? What gifts or cards do you send each quarter or holiday season? Once you've defined it, turn it into a system you can follow with joy and ease. And if you're not a systems person? Delegate it. You're not building a database, you're building a legacy of care.

Why Presence Beats Perfection 🏆

Passive marketing keeps you *present,* even when you're not actively marketing. That's powerful.

You don't have to be flashy or post daily on social media. You just need to show up *consistently*. Passive strategies support this. They remind past clients why they love you and give future clients a reason to trust you.

When your branding is unified across your business cards, your website, your mailings, and your social channels, even subtly, it builds a feeling of reliability. And that is the golden ingredient in any referral-based business.

⬤ Be the Brand They Remember

Here's the truth: the most successful agents aren't constantly chasing. **They're consistently showing up**. Not in a flashy, frantic way, but in a steady, soul-aligned rhythm that says, *"I'm here. I care. I've got you."*

When you build a brand with intention and infuse your marketing materials with care, people begin to recognize you, not just as an agent, but as **someone they can trust**.

Client follow-up systems aren't just business tools, they're relationship builders. They say, *"You matter to me,"* without requiring you to be glued to your phone at all times. Whether you're using a simple spreadsheet, an elegant CRM, or a full-service program, what matters is that you **create repeatable systems**. Ones that let you nurture leads, serve current clients, and stay present in the lives of your past clients long after the keys have been handed over.

This is the heartbeat of passive marketing done right. You're not waiting around, you're planting seeds. And over time, those seeds bloom into relationships, referrals, and a business built on trust and visibility.

So, keep showing up — consistently, and authentically. Because when people are finally ready to make a move, they'll remember the agent who didn't just sell homes, but showed up with heart.

🔑 Key Reflections

What passive marketing strategies do I currently use ?
And how can I make that presence more intentional and
aligned with my brand?

_____

_____

_____

_____

_____

_____

What client care system *(spreadsheet, Notion, CRM,
mailing calendar, etc.)* would best support me in staying
connected before, during, and after a transaction?

_____

_____

_____

What small touches could I automate or systematize to
keep my business personal, even when I'm not present?

_____

_____

_____

_____

_____

NOTES

DOODLES

CHAPTER 6

The MAGIC of ACTIVE Marketing

Active marketing is where your visibility meets real-world connection. It's not just about handing out business cards or showing up at events. It's about **becoming a trusted presence in your community** and in the lives of your clients. Active strategies build momentum. They create buzz, deepen relationships, and keep you at the top of heart.

In a world where inboxes overflow and algorithms change by the hour, there's something timeless and powerful about being physically present; showing up with a smile, lending a hand, or surprising someone with a thoughtful gesture. These small, consistent actions become the heartbeat of your brand. You don't just *tell* people you care. You *show* them.

Shine your light so the right people can find you.

🛍️ Pop-Bys, Networking, and Events - with Intention

Pop-bys are more than just a branded goodie bag or seasonal treat. When done with intention, they're meaningful touchpoints that say, *"I'm thinking of you."*

Whether it's a spring flower with a tag that says, *"Planting roots?"* or a pumpkin pie at Thanksgiving, with a note that reads, *"I am so <u>thankful</u> for you!"* a well-timed pop-by can be personal, memorable, and appreciated.

And it doesn't stop there. **Community networking events,** especially ones where you're volunteering, co-hosting, or simply showing up as a cheerleader, allow you to connect with your sphere naturally.

The key? Be a giver. Bring value.
Ask about others first. Every event you attend *(or create!)* is an opportunity to leave someone feeling good just because they talked to you.

Keep the focus on the person you are speaking with. Ask questions about themselves and they will come away feeling awesome.

- *"Tell me something fun you've done lately. I love to live vicariously through my friends' adventures!"*
- *"How are the kids/grandkids doing? What activities are they into these days?"*
- *"What's lighting you up these days? Tell me about something that is bringing you joy."*
- *"Read any good books or seen any great movies lately? That sounds great! I'll be sure to check it out."*

Client appreciation events also work wonders. These don't have to be expensive or elaborate. A cozy coffee morning, ice cream social, or mini pumpkin patch in your driveway can create priceless goodwill. It's not about perfection. It's about presence.

PRO TIP

Piggyback your efforts on a holiday that is already happening. Set up a living room in the driveway on Halloween; with chairs, rug, fire, heaters, and give away dollar store toys and gifts. Parents sit for a bit, the kids choose their BIG treats, and you get lots of photos for social media marketing. It's a win-win for everyone!

How to Ask for Business ❓

Let's be honest: no one wants to sound pushy, aggressive, or smarmy. And good news! You don't have to. You can ask for business with warmth and confidence:

- *"I love helping awesome people like you. If you know someone buying or selling, I'd be honored to help."*

- *"You know how I work. I take care of my people like they're family. If anyone in your circle needs that kind of support right now in buying or selling a home, I hope you'll send them my way."*

- *"I just wanted to say thank you again for your support. Whether it's sharing kind words, a referral, or simply cheering me on, you have always been the BEST."*

When you lead with service and follow up with clarity, your message feels like an invitation, not a pitch. And when it's backed by **genuine connection and consistent care**, people want to use you... and refer you.

📱 Social Shout-Outs and Unexpected Client Care

Your social media isn't just a digital billboard, it's a relationship builder. Share highlights from your events. Celebrate your clients. Cheer on local businesses. *"Advertise"* your partners and collaborators by telling people about what they do *and* why you love them.

These shout-outs are more than just kind gestures. They're strategic visibility. They show that you're active, engaged, and community focused. Plus, people love being seen and appreciated. And they often share your posts, widening your reach without a single ad dollar spent.

Add in unexpected moments of care, like a happy anniversary message, a birthday card, or a quick text to check in, and you've got a client care strategy that stands out from the crowd.

- **Send a meme of something they enjoy.** *"Hi [Name], I saw this amazing library she shed and thought of you. Hope life's treating you kindly. Let me know if there's ever anything I can do to support you!"*

- **Send a photo of them at their closing.** *"Hey! Happy one-year anniversary for your home! I hope you are loving it so much!"*

- **Send them a picture of their house.** *"Hi [Name], I was nearby your neighborhood and smiled thinking of your adorable home. Hope all is well — sending warm wishes your way!"*

📅 Seasonal Marketing: Staying Relevant All Year

The seasons offer natural opportunities to stay in touch. From January's "new year, fresh start" energy to December's cozy gratitude, each month brings a chance to show up with something timely and thoughtful.

Ideas for Spring:

- Send Market updates, garden tips, or *"clean up your mortgage"* check-ins
- Post *"before and after"* landscaping inspiration for curb appeal

Ideas for Summer:

- Host an ice cream social or barbecue
- Create a downloadable local summer fun guide *(free events, hikes, museums, splash pads)*

Ideas for Autumn:

- Post back-to-school routines and home workspace inspiration
- Mini pies, football-themed pop-bys, or *"fall in love with your home"* messages

Ideas for Winter:

- Holiday drop-offs, home prep tips, or warm wishes sent with cocoa and joy
- Host a Snowman Building Contest and have entrants send you photos; prizes for biggest, funniest, most traditional, most creative

You can create a calendar of outreach so that you never run out of reasons to connect.

How to Actively Serve Your Sphere and Stay Top of Heart ♥

Ultimately, active marketing is about nurturing relationships. It's showing your people that you're not just in real estate, you're in *relationship estate*. You care about their milestones, their families, their wins, and their lives beyond the transaction.

Start by identifying your top **25 or 50 VIPs;** clients, referral partners, neighbors, and connectors, and create a plan to stay in touch. Aim for quarterly pop-bys, regular check-ins, and occasional wow moments. You'll be amazed at the ripple effect.

> You don't have to do it all at once. Just **pick one action** you can take this week. then let your magic grow from there.

WOW YOUR VIPS!

⟨⬦⟩ Consistent Action = Meaningful Momentum

Active marketing isn't about burning yourself out trying to be everywhere. It's about choosing the places, people, and practices that light you up, and showing up consistently.

When you lean into relationships with generosity and joy, you don't have to chase leads. They find you. Your pop-bys spark smiles. Your notes create loyalty. Your events deepen connection. Bit by bit, step by step, you build something far more powerful than a marketing campaign. You create a community that loves to spend time with you, use you for real estate, and refer you to people *they* care about.

🔑 Key Reflections

Which active marketing strategy feels the most natural and joyful for me to do consistently?

_____

_____

_____

_____

_____

Who are three people in my sphere I can reach out to this week just to connect, appreciate, or celebrate?

_____

_____

_____

_____

_____

What seasonal or community-inspired ideas could I bring to life this quarter to stay visible and top of heart?

_____

_____

_____

_____

_____

NOTES

CHAPTER 7

Social Media
Without the STRESS

> Marketing is simply sharing what you love with people who need it.

Social media can feel like both a blessing and a burden. It's a free marketing tool that puts your brand in front of people every day, but it can also be exhausting, overwhelming, and... let's be honest, sometimes even demoralizing.

But here's the good news: You don't need to be viral. You don't need to dance, point to bubbles, or share your entire life online. What you *do* need is a presence that reflects who you are, what you stand for, and how you serve.

Let's take the pressure off and bring the joy back in.

Choose Platforms That Suit Your Strengths

Not all social media platforms are created equal. And not all of them are for you. Instead of feeling like you need to be *everywhere*, focus on being **somewhere with intention.**

- If you love connecting with people directly and having conversations, Facebook might be your jam.
- If you enjoy visuals and storytelling, Instagram is perfect.
- Prefer sharing market tips or longer posts? LinkedIn may be your space.
- Short bursts of inspiration? Threads or X (Twitter) could be fun.
- Pinterest is fantastic for evergreen content.
- YouTube works wonders if you're a natural talker or love showing homes on video.

Ask yourself:

- Where do my ideal clients hang out?
- What platform do I actually enjoy using?
- Where can I show up consistently?

The key is alignment. You're building *your* brand, so lean into platforms that support your personality and business goals.

What to Post When You Don't Want to Dance or Overshare

You're not here to entertain. You're here to *connect*. And yes, you can connect powerfully without ever dancing, pointing, or lip-syncing in a social media post *(unless you are a born performer and love this kind of posting... then go for it).*

Here are some stress-free post ideas that feel natural and grounded:

- A story about a recent client win *(with permission or change the name of the client in the story)*
- A photo of your workspace with a caption about today's to-do list
- A behind-the-scenes look at an open house setup
- A community highlight *(favorite café, event, or mural)*
- A market tip explained in everyday language
- A simple quote graphic that reflects your brand values
- A throwback photo from when you started in real estate
- A client shout-out or testimonial

The magic lies in being relatable, real, and showing up consistently. When people see the real you; your warmth, your passion, your quirks, and your caring, they feel a connection that can't be manufactured.

It's not about perfection or performance; **it's about presence.** Show up with your true voice, your genuine joy, and your everyday moments, and you'll create a ripple of recognition and trust.

When you share regularly, and from the heart, your audience starts to feel like they know you. And that's when the genius of connection turns into the magic of conversion.

Focus on Intention Over Virality ◉

Forget about chasing algorithms. What builds **trust and connection** over time isn't the one post that reaches thousands, it's the quiet, steady rhythm of showing up week after week.

That might mean posting three times a week, once a day, or just once a week. Whatever cadence fits your flow, honor it. If it helps, **create content in batches**. Use a tool like Canva, Later, or Meta Business Suite to schedule ahead. That way, your marketing runs while you live your life.

> ✦ **A steady presence builds familiarity.**
> ♡ ✳ **And familiarity builds trust.**

✋ Set Boundaries So Social Stays Sustainable

Social media is meant to serve you, not drain you. Set boundaries that help you stay energized, not depleted. Posting regularly, especially on more than one platform, can sometimes feel a little overwhelming.

Here are a few gentle reminders:

- Schedule screen-free hours or days.
- Unfollow accounts that make you feel like you're not enough.
- Decide in advance how much time you'll spend engaging.
- Don't feel pressured to respond instantly.
- Let go of likes as a measure of your value.

You are building a heart-centered business, not a highlight reel. And *your* real magic is happening offline; in your relationships, your service, and the moments no one sees.

Show Up and Shine – Your Way ☀️

Social media is simply a microphone. And when you use it with heart, intention, and a steady flow, it amplifies *your* voice, *your* values, and *your* vision.

You don't need to be the loudest. You just need to be you, showing up with love, intention, and a touch of sparkle.

Let your posts reflect your personality.

Let your presence feel like a warm invitation.

Let your feed be a celebration of what you have to offer.

You've got this, and your people are out there, watching, smiling, and feeling grateful that you're the one they're following.

🔑 Key Reflections

Which social media platform feels most aligned with my energy, style, and message? And why?

_____

_____

_____

_____

_____

What kinds of posts feel easy, fun, and authentic for me to share regularly?

_____

_____

_____

_____

_____

How can I create a sustainable rhythm for showing up online that supports my business and protects my peace?

_____

_____

_____

_____

_____

NOTES

DOODLES

CHAPTER 8

Create a CONTENT PLAN You Can COMMIT to Using

So many agents want to post on social media. They know it matters. They know it is

> *Promoting your gifts invites others to grow through them.*

important. They know it helps with visibility and brand recognition. But then life gets busy, listings need attention, a deal goes sideways... and social media falls to the bottom of the to-do list. Sound familiar?

If you've ever opened up Instagram with the best of intentions and then wasted 30 minutes scrolling instead of sharing, you are not alone. The key isn't about being everywhere or perfect. It's about having a plan that supports you, not stresses you out.

Let's build a content system that feels good, reflects who you are, and actually gets done.

The Foundation: A Weekly or Monthly Map

A content plan doesn't need to be complicated. **It needs to be sustainable**. Start with what you know: how often can you realistically show up? If it's once a week, great. If it's three times a week, even better. But the magic is in the rhythm, not the volume.

Here's a simple 4-post weekly schedule you can adapt:

- **Monday**: *Motivation or Personal Insight* – Share a quote, a client story, or a behind-the-scenes reflection.
- **Wednesday**: *Real Estate Tip* – Teach your audience something helpful: market update, staging advice, loan info.
- **Friday**: *Fun or Lifestyle Post* – Feature a local business, a home decor tip, or even your adorable dog.
- **Sunday**: *Spotlight or Promo* – A *"Just Sold"* or *"New Listing"* post, client testimonial, or reminder of your services.

You can also scale this rhythm monthly. For example, Week 1 could be educational, Week 2 personal, Week 3 promotional, and Week 4 lifestyle-focused.

You're not locked in. This a living, breathing plan that can shift with you. The goal is not to pressure you, but to support you.

Mix Personal, Professional, and Promotional Content

Gone are the days when people only want polished real estate professional exposure. Your audience wants to know *you*. They want to trust you. They want to feel connected before they ever reach out for a home search or listing consultation.

Think of your content as a conversation, not a commercial. Use the **3 P's formula**:

- **Personal** – Share moments from your life: family, hobbies, travel, lessons learned.
- **Professional** – Talk about your process, what you love about real estate, or share *"a day in the life."*
- **Promotional** – Highlight listings, services, buyer wins, seller success stories.

Each category serves a purpose. And when they're all present, your brand feels whole, honest, and magnetic.

Save Time with Canva Templates & Batching

You don't need to design from scratch every time. Online design platforms like Canva make it easy to create on-brand posts in minutes. Canva has ready-made templates for property flyers, social media posts, signs, event announcements, and more. If you have never used Canva, you can easily learn with their tutorials or videos on YouTube. *(I use Canva and luuuuuuv it!)* Choose a few templates that reflect your look and feel; maybe soft neutrals, modern black-and-white, or playful pops of color, and reuse them.

Batch Your Content

Set aside 1–2 hours a week to work *"on your business"* to create and schedule your social media posts. Use free tools like Meta Business Suite, Later, or Planoly to plan ahead and save time. You can design all of your posts for the week and then schedule them to post throughout the week. This will allow you the freedom to work *"in your business."*

Repurpose to Maximize Your Magic

When you are creating marketing content or items of value, also use these items as social media posts.

- Your **email newsletter**? That's a post.
- Your **open house video**? Break it into reels.
- Your **buyer guide**? Turn tips into bite-sized graphics.

Repurposing is about making your content work harder for you — not creating more. If something resonates on one platform, there's a good chance it will connect elsewhere.

Keep a **Content Goldmine** doc or folder where you save all your ideas, past posts, and great wording. When you're having an off day, that bank of brilliance will carry you.

PRO TIP Create a folder of evergreen captions and hashtags. Rotate them in with new photos or designs. Most people won't remember, but you'll always be showing up with value.

🎤 Your Voice, Your Plan, Your Way

You don't need to be a content wizard, a social media influencer, or a full-time marketer to meaningfully show up for your audience. You just need to be *you,* working a plan that supports your rhythm and lifestyle.

Your content doesn't have to be perfect, polished, or performative. It simply needs to be real, relevant, and reflective of who you are. When your posts are infused with your voice and values, people feel that. They don't scroll past. They pause. They smile. They think of you the next time someone mentions buying or selling.

The beauty of a content plan isn't in the posts themselves, it's in the peace of mind that comes from knowing you're staying visible without burning out. When you have a content plan, a few favorite templates, and a stash of ideas ready to go, **you eliminate decision fatigue and free up energy** for the parts of your business (and life!) that light you up.

This is where your content becomes your compass. Each post is a subtle reminder to your community that you're still here, still serving, and still showing up with heart.

Whether you're sharing a new listing, a behind-the-scenes moment, or a happy client celebration, it all adds up to a brand that's attractive and memorable.

And the best part? You can make it fun! Let your voice shine. Let your creativity play. And let your content be a natural extension of your brilliance.

🔑 Key Reflections

What types of posts *(personal, professional, promotional)* do I naturally gravitate toward. Which ones do I avoid?

_____

_____

_____

_____

_____

What could my weekly or monthly content plan look like?

_____

_____

_____

_____

_____

_____

Where can I simplify or automate my content creation to make it more easier and more consistent?

_____

_____

_____

_____

_____

NOTES

DOODLES

Create MORE Energetic
ENGAGEMENT

Your goal is not to be a social media star or to slide into every DM with a pitch in order to build a thriving real estate business. In fact, the most magnetic kind of marketing

Being seen is a service, not a spotlight.

isn't a strategy, **it's a connection**. The most impactful agents are the ones who show up with heart, with presence, and with genuine interest in other people's lives.

We are talking now about *engagement*. Not in the buzzwordy way, but in the human-to-human, smile-through-the-screen, cheer-for-your-friends kind of way. It's about crafting online interactions that feel just as good as your real-life ones. Because when you engage with soul *(instead of spam)*, you're not just creating content. **You're creating community**.

Build Genuine Relationships Online 🧑‍🤝‍🧑

If you wouldn't walk up to someone in line at the grocery store and shout, *"Do you want to sell your house?"* you won't want to do that online either. Digital relationship-building is about the same principles that work in the real world: **listen more than you talk, be kind, be helpful, be curious.**

Here's how that looks in action:

- Instead of dropping links, ask questions.
- Instead of pushing listings, share a behind-the-scenes look at the day you staged the home or the moment your client got the keys.
- Instead of cold DMs, leave thoughtful comments on other people's posts, or send them heartfelt DMs. Congratulate them on their kid's graduation. Compliment their dog. Be a real human.

Remember: social media is not just a megaphone, it's a dinner party. Show up like you would to your favorite gathering; warm, interested, and eager to celebrate others.

🎉 The Power of Comments, DMs & Celebrations

Want to turn online followers into raving fans? **Make them feel seen.** It takes almost no time to leave a meaningful comment. But that moment of acknowledgement can spark a whole new relationship. A comment like *"I love this idea!"* or *"This made me smile!"* builds more goodwill than a hundred generic hearts or "likes."

And when it comes to DMs, don't wait for the perfect moment or a salesy opener.

- Send a voice note telling someone how much you enjoyed their latest post.
- Drop a happy birthday message.
- Cheer on their wins.
- Ask about their new kitten.

These micro-moments are what create macro-trust. Celebrating others authentically is one of the most beneficial things you can do for your business. Help people feel appreciated and supported, and you'll build a reputation as someone they want to work with.

💬 Create Conversations That Matter

Stories, polls, and live videos are not just *"content features,"* they're conversation starters. They invite people into your world and give them a chance to participate. **That's engagement magic.**

Try simple, soul-aligned prompts like:

- *"What's one small win you had today?"*
- *"Would you rather live in the mountains or by the beach?"*
- *"Guess how many cookies I just ate at my open house today?"*

You're not aiming for perfection. **You're aiming for connection**. The more real and relatable you are, the more people feel invited to interact.

And don't forget to respond when they do. Every vote, every comment, every emoji reaction is a human choosing to engage with you.

Treat this like the gold that it is.

⚡ The Energy Behind Engagement: Why Your Vibe Matters

Your content builds awareness, but your engagement builds trust. And trust turns someone who sees your posts into someone who calls you when it's time to buy or sell.

It's not just what you say online, it's the energy behind it. **When you show up with genuine care, joy, and curiosity, your people feel it.** Whether you're replying to a comment, leaving a thoughtful DM, or sharing a story about your day, the vibration you bring creates a ripple effect. Thoughtful engagement means you're not trying to get something, You're offering something: kindness, encouragement, connection.

Think of your social media as a sacred space where energy flows both ways. The more heart-centered energy you pour into it, the more your community will respond with loyalty, trust, and referrals.

This is the magic of authentic connection.

- It's the smile behind the message.
- The warmth behind the words.
- The presence behind the post.

✦ Let your vibe do the heavy lifting and ✦ you'll never feel like you're "selling" again. ♡

Engagement isn't about performing. It's about participating. And when you participate with intention, you create relationships that ripple far beyond the screen.

Make It About Them

The most powerful kind of online marketing is the kind that's not about you at all. It's about creating a space where others feel seen, heard, and valued. When you shift from *"How can I get more business?"* to *"How can I make more connections?"* The business comes naturally.

So go ahead. Scroll with intention. Comment with kindness. Message with meaning. Show up in your feed like you would in your favorite cafe; full of heart, ready to say hello, and excited to see who's there.

🗝️ Key Reflections

Where can I show up more consistently with heart online, not just to promote, but to connect?

_____

_____

_____

_____

_____

What small, soulful touches can I add to my weekly engagement to make others feel seen and appreciated?

_____

_____

_____

_____

_____

How can I turn followers into true fans by inviting more conversation and connection into my posts and stories?

_____

_____

_____

_____

_____

NOTES

DOODLES

CHAPTER 10

Keep UP the
MOMENTUM

> ⭐
> *Gain momentum by adding moments of success achieved.*

You've done so much good already. You've clarified your message, shown up with purpose, crafted content that feels aligned, and found joy in both passive and active marketing strategies.

Now what? ... You keep going.

Not at a frantic pace. Not from pressure or panic. You keep up your momentum from a grounded, heart-aligned place that trusts that **momentum builds magic.**

Stay Consistent - Even When Life Gets Busy 📈

Consistency doesn't have to be flawless. It's about showing up regularly, in whatever capacity you can, to nurture your visibility and connection with your audience. But let's be real: there are weeks when you're busy with clients, putting out fires, or simply not feeling inspired. That's okay!

Instead of disappearing altogether, **scale your efforts**. Post a quick photo with a short caption. Send one check-in text to a past client. Comment on three social media posts from people in your sphere. **Consistency is a rhythm, not a race**.

Keep a handful of *"backup"* posts ready to go; quotes, photos, evergreen tips, that you can use in a pinch. And when energy returns, ride that wave and create a little extra content to stockpile. Your future self will thank you.

Refresh Without Reinventing

There's a temptation to think you need to constantly do something new. New branding, new bio, new slogan, new format. But often, your message simply needs a little polish, not a full makeover.

Take a moment every few months to review your content.

- Is my messaging still aligned with my goals and values?
- Are there ways to simplify or clarify what I offer?
- Could I reuse or reframe some past content for a fresh feel?

Sometimes, refreshing your message is as simple as updating the visuals, tweaking a headline, or adding a new photo. Don't let *"shiny object syndrome"* pull you off your path. What you're building is already beautiful.

Build a Marketing Plan You Enjoy

Marketing doesn't have to be overwhelming, or one-size-fits-all. The key is to create a plan that lights you up and works with your energy, not against it. A plan that feels good is one you'll actually follow, even when life gets full or you hit a slow season.

Yes, social media plays a role. But it's only one piece of a bigger, more beautiful puzzle. Your marketing strategy can *(and should)* include passive marketing tools that keep working in the background. Think: your business card, email signature, printed newsletters, website, community flyers, auto-drip campaigns, mailers, signage, and branded gifts. These may not be flashy, but they build long-term awareness and presence in subtle, soul-aligned ways.

Now pair that with active marketing; those high-touch, high-heart strategies that show you're present, invested, and available. This might mean attending local networking events, hosting seasonal pop-bys, participating in community fundraisers, or creating client appreciation experiences. Even something as simple as writing personal notes or dropping off a cute treat can keep you visible in a meaningful way.

When you mix both passive and active strategies, along with social content that reflects your true self, you end up with a marketing plan that's sustainable, soulful, and strategic. The best part? You're no longer guessing what to do next. You've created a rhythm you can repeat; one that feels like you and delivers results you can trust.

👍 Keep Showing Up

The real magic in marketing isn't found in a viral reel or a flashy billboard. It's found in the **easeful, steady flow of showing up with heart.** It's the handwritten note you send after a showing, the kind words you speak at a community event, and the authentic story you share online that makes someone feel seen. When you show up with purpose, you create connection. And connection is what keeps your brand alive in the hearts and minds of those you serve.

Staying visible means finding your favorite ways to be of service and choosing consistency over chaos. It's about building a marketing plan that reflects your energy, supports your life, and grows your business in a way that is aligned.

No matter the season, the market, or the mood you're in, **let your message be a lighthouse.** Keep showing up. Not to prove something, but to share something. Let your presence be a gift. Over time, it builds trust. Over time, it builds a brand. And over time, it builds a business that not only provides, it fulfills.

🔑 Key Reflections

What rhythms, routines, or marketing actions feel sustainable and enjoyable in this season?

_____

_____

_____

_____

_____

Where in my business or message could I refresh or simplify without starting from scratch?

_____

_____

_____

_____

_____

When was the last time I celebrated how far I've come?

_____

_____

_____

_____

_____

Pause. Acknowledge your growth. You're doing amazing. Truly.

NOTES

You Are a MARKETING MAGNET

Marketing can sometimes feel like a chore, or worse, a performance. But in reality, it's something much deeper, much more powerful. It's about showing up so the right people can find you. It's about letting your presence, your light, do the talking before you even open your mouth.

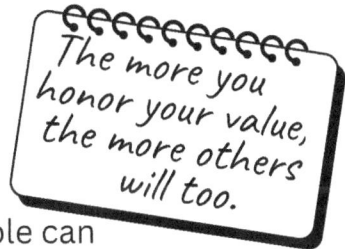

> The more you honor your value, the more others will too.

Because the truth is, you're not just a real estate agent with a catchy slogan. You are a living, breathing invitation. **You're not just marketing... you're magnetizing.**

Marketing Is About Being Seen So People Can Choose You

Too often, marketing gets reduced to algorithms, ad budgets, and trying to "crack the code" of the latest trend. But the heart of marketing, the soul of it, is visibility. When people see you, not just your listings or logos, but the real you, they can connect. And when they connect, they can choose.

This isn't about being the loudest or most polished. It's about being present. When you show up consistently *(with warmth, authenticity, and heart)*, you begin to stand out. Not because you shouted louder, but because you resonated deeper.

Visibility isn't vanity. It's service. When you stay visible, you stay available to the people who need you most.

You Are Worthy of Being Visible, Valued, and Chosen

Let's pause here for a moment. It can be uncomfortable to market yourself; to post that video, send that email, or show up to that networking event. But underneath the hesitation is often a deeper fear: *What if I'm not enough?*

You *are* enough. You are worthy of being seen. You are worthy of being valued. You are worthy of being chosen, and referred, and celebrated, and remembered.

Authentic marketing is about owning that worthiness. It's about believing in your value so deeply that you don't shrink from the spotlight. You shine in it. And when you do, you give your clients permission to trust you, to lean in, and to say,

"Yes, I want to work with you."

✦ The Right Clients Are Looking for You – ✦ Let Them See Your Light

Somewhere out there, right now, someone is scrolling, searching, asking a friend, wondering: Who can I trust with this huge life decision?

This is the heart of **attraction-based marketing**: the belief that when you stand in your truth, when you radiate your values, when you simply show up with love and service, the people who need you can find you. They will feel that spark. They will recognize your light.

So, whether you're posting a listing, writing a newsletter, chatting at a barbecue, or waving from your car, you are marketing. And you are attracting. You are the gentle tap on the shoulder that says, *"I'm here. I've got you."*

Shine Like Only You Can ☀

You don't have to chase every lead. You don't have to follow every trend. You don't have to pretend to be someone you're not.

Just keep showing up as the real you; in your joy, your service, your magic. Be visible. Be vibrant. Be vocal about who you are and how you can help.

You *are* absolutely, just exactly what they need.

Donna ♡

NOTES

MORE MAGIC

I just couldn't end this guide without adding a few extra ideas to help you build your referral and rewards system for your business. I hope you enjoy these bonus ideas.

BONUS: Dream Client Avatar

Your dream clients are out there. When you define them clearly, you can speak directly to them, show up where they are, and build a brand that naturally attracts them.

Take a few quiet moments to reflect, dream, and write from the heart.

Who Are They?

- Name your Dream Client
- Age Range
- Profession or Lifestyle
- Are they single, married, retired, newly relocated?
- What stage of life are they in?
- First home? Upsizing? Downsizing? Investing?

How Do They Think and Speak?

- What are 3 things they worry about when buying or selling?
- What do they wish their agent would do or understand?
- What questions do they ask most often?
- What kind of communication style do they prefer?

What Do They Want?

- What are their real estate goals or dreams?
- What do they value most in an agent?
- What experience are they hoping for?

Why Will They Choose YOU?

- What makes you a perfect fit for this person?
- How will you show up in a way that makes them feel seen, heard, and supported?
- What special touches or services will feel extra meaningful to them?

BONUS: Branding Checklist

Your brand isn't just your logo. It's the feeling people have when they think of you. It's how you show up, the message you share, and the energy you bring. Use this checklist to ensure your brand is on point.

My Mission Statement

_____

_____

_____

_____

_____

_____

Brand Clarity

___ I know who my Dream Client is
___ I have a clear mission statement or tagline
___ I can describe my vibe or personality in 3 words
___ My messaging reflects my values and vision
___ I've chosen a few signature phrases or slogans to use

Visual Identity

___ I've selected a consistent color palette
___ I use 1–2 fonts regularly across all platforms
___ I have a logo *(or name styling)* that feels like me
___ My Canva templates match my brand style
___ My images and graphics feel cohesive

Voice and Vibe

___ My posts and marketing materials sound like me
___ I've identified my brand tone *(fun, professional, warm, etc.)*
___ I write in a way that's relatable and real
___ I've created content that builds trust and connection
___ My brand makes people feel a specific emotion *(ex: calm, inspired, empowered)*

Brand Touchpoints

___ My email signature includes my branding elements
___ My website / landing page feels like an extension of me
___ My online bios clearly reflect my values and niche
___ My business cards/flyers match my brand style
___ My pop-bys, thank you gifts, and client experiences reflect my brand personality

Brand Magic

__ I've infused my brand with heart and purpose
__ I've created a few *"wow"* moments for my clients
__ I'm consistent, not robotic, real over perfect
__ My marketing makes me feel proud, seen, and aligned
__ I trust that my brand is attracting the right people into
     my world

♥ BONUS: SOI Connections Schedule

One of the best methods I have found for keeping in touch with my Sphere of Influence is to ensure contact and visibility several times per month. Here is a sample schedule showing how many connections I use and what kinds of contact:

January 1: **Postcard Mailer** - Winter Home Checklist
January 15: **E-Newsletter** - Tax Tips
January 25: **SOI Phone Call** - New Year Check In
February 1: **Postcard Mailer** - Love Affirmations
February 5: **Holiday Text** - Happy Valentine's Day
          Branded Graphic
February 20: **E-Newsletter** - Last Quarter Market Report
March 1: **Postcard Mailer** - Happy St. Patrick's Day
March 15: **E-Newsletter** - Spring Home Checklist
March 25: **Client Appreciation Event Invite Mailer** -
          Easter Egg Hunt

April 1: **Phone Call** - Easter Egg Hunt Invitation
April 2: **Postcard Mailer** - Gardening Tips
April 7: **Reminder Text** - Easter Egg Hunt Branded Graphic
April 15: **E-Newsletter** - Home Decor Tips
May 1: **Postcard Mailer** - May Flowers Fun
May 15: **E-Newsletter** - 1st Quarter Market Report
June 1: **Postcard Maile**r - Local Summer Fun Activities
June 15: **E-Newsletter** - Summer Vacation Tips
July 1: **Postcard Mailer** - Fireworks Safety Guide
July 15: **E-Newsletter** - Home Staging Tips
August 1: **Postcard Mailer** - Tax Appeal Information
August 8: **Phone Call** - Tax Appeal Discussion
August 15: **E-Newsletter** - Back to School Tips
September 1: **Postcard Mailer** - Autumn Fun
September 15: **E-Newsletter** - 2nd Quarter Market Report
September 25: **Event Invite Mailer** - Pumpkin Patch Party
October 1: **Postcard Mailer** - Fall Home Decor Ideas
October 5: **Reminder Text** - Pumpkin Patch Party
                        Branded Graphic
October 15: **E-Newsletter** - Halloween Safety Tips
November 1: **Postcard Mailer** - Save the Date for Pies
November 10: **Newsletter** - with Gratitude Tips
November 20: **Reminder Text** - Thanksgiving Mini Pies
            Branded Graphic
December 1: **Postcard Mailer** -
        Holiday Fun Ideas
December 15: **E-Newsletter** -
        Holiday Tips
December 17: **Phone Call** -
    Holiday Season Love
December 24: **Happy Holidays
    Text** - Branded Graphic

BONUS: Seller and Buyer Lead Follow Up Campaigns

Create Follow Up Action Plans are for continuing communication and showing your expertise. Design and load your emails and scripts into your CRM system or make a checklist to add to each of your new client files.

Follow Up for Seller Leads

Day 1: **Email** - It Was So Wonderful Meeting You
Day 8: **Email** - Know What to Ask Before You Make a Move
Day 15: **Email** - FREE Home Review E-Book for Sellers
Day 22: **Email** - Ensure Homebuyers LOVE Your Home
Day 29: **Email** - Homebuyers Want to Know Your Home
Day 30: **Phone Call** - Friendly Check In
Day 36: **Email** - The Real Estate Market Has Changed
Day 43: **Email** - Find Out What Your Home Is Worth
Day 50: **Email** - I Am Your Community Connection
Day 57: **Email** - Pricing Your Home to Sell
Day 64: **Email** - The Home Selling Process Defined
Day 65: **Phone Call** - Friendly Check In

Follow Up for Buyer Leads

Day 1: **Email** - It Was So Wonderful Meeting You
Day 8: **Email** - Did You Know... The Seller Pays Me
Day 15: **Email** - Know About Extra Costs Before Buying
Day 22: **Email** - Tips to Improve Your Credit Score
Day 29: **Email** - Save Money When You Buy a Home
Day 30: **Phone Call** - Friendly Check In
Day 36: **Email** - Know About Mortgages Before You Buy
Day 43: **Email** - I Am Your Community Connection
Day 50: **Email** - Ways to Save for a Down Payment
Day 57: **Email** - Stop Renting and Own Your Own Home
Day 64: **Email** - Buying a Home Should Be Exciting & Fun!
Day 65: **Phone Call** - Friendly Check In

BONUS: Social Media Prompts for Creating Posts

These are prompts for creating engagement and visibility. Include photos or branded graphics with your posts. You want to ensure that your social media friends continue to follow you, so don't make it all about business. Be sure to create balance by adding plenty of personal posts in between.

- Share your 'why' for being in real estate.
- Introduce yourself with a fun fact not on your bio.
- Post a behind-the-scenes photo of your day.
- Celebrate a recent client success story.
- Share your favorite coffee shop or workspace.
- Highlight a local small business you love.
- Post a testimonial or review from a happy client.
- Share a tip for first-time homebuyers.
- Talk about what makes your neighborhood special.
- Ask your audience what they love most about their home.
- Do a gratitude post for clients or mentors.
- Celebrate a team member or referral partner.
- Show a before-and-after of a listing or project.
- Give a sneak peek of something you're working on.
- Share a quote that inspires your business mindset.
- Do a "This or That" poll about home features.
- Talk about how you support clients after the sale.
- Highlight a community event or charity you support.
- Post a fun "Did You Know" real estate fact.
- Share your favorite way to unwind after a long day.
- Show off your pop-by or client gift ideas.
- Explain a common real estate myth and the truth.
- Share a seasonal home maintenance or decor tip.
- Tell a story about how you got started in real estate.

❤ BONUS: Nourishing Practices for the Magnetic You

Your energy is your greatest marketing tool. And that energy needs replenishing, nurturing, and care — especially when you're actively showing up online, in person, and everywhere in between.

Visibility is powerful, but it's also vulnerable. It asks us to be present, creative, generous, and responsive. Let's make sure you're filling your own well as beautifully as you're pouring into others.

This isn't about spa days *(though yes, please!)*. This is about daily rituals that support your nervous system, nurture your creativity, and protect your peace.

Protect Your Morning Energy
Begin your day for *you* before the world takes over. A few deep breaths, a cup of tea, journaling; anything that grounds you.

Use Digital Boundaries
Visibility doesn't mean 24/7 access. Create intentional social media check-ins instead of all-day scrolling. Unplug without guilt.

Celebrate Quiet Wins
Not every success is loud or likes-driven. A kind message from a client, a thoughtful comment count those as magic.

Create Before You Consume
Start your content or your workday with your voice, your ideas, your creativity. Then check email or social.

Make Movement a Marketing Ritual
Walking, dancing, stretching; when your body feels alive, so does your messaging.

Say No with Grace
Not all opportunities are aligned. So, every *"no"* can be a "yes" to your peace, your purpose, and your people.

Surround Yourself with Light-Filled People
You don't need a huge circle. You need an energizing one. Your vibe tribe matters.

Create Off-Camera Days
You're allowed to be visible without being seen. Rest from the camera and the spotlight when needed.

Check in with Yourself
"What do I need right now?" is a powerful marketing question. Because if you're out of alignment, your audience will feel it too.

Remember Your Why
Visibility is not vanity. It's service. You're here to help, guide, support, and uplift. And that's sacred.

You don't have to do it all, be everywhere, or be everything to everyone. You just need to be the version of you that feels real, radiant, and replenished. When you care for your energy, your marketing becomes magnetic. Because your light shines brighter and truer than ever.

NOTES

NOTES

NOTES

NOTES

NOTES

NOTES

NOTES

NOTES

ABOUT THE AUTHOR

Donna Wysinger began her real estate career over 25 years ago with a simple curiosity about flipping homes. What started as a personal interest quickly grew into helping friends and family buy and sell properties.

Though she hadn't planned on becoming a full-time Realtor, Donna soon realized that true success would only come by trusting herself and going all in. She immersed herself in the industry, learning every aspect of the business while working alongside top agents and on highly successful teams. Over the years she has worn many hats: listing specialist, buyer guide, transaction coordinator, admin support, new homes specialist, marketing designer and coordinator, new agents trainer, new assistants trainer, and more.

With her strong background in design and marketing, Donna also helped countless agents grow their businesses by creating resources and tools that helped them stand out. Eventually, she partnered with her sister to build a thriving real estate business of her own, using the very systems and strategies she had been developing and teaching. Together, they built not only sales, but lasting relationships within their community.

Today, after more than a quarter century in the industry, Donna has distilled her knowledge and experience into the **Be a Better Agent** community and her series of quick-read guidebooks. Her mission is simple: to help real estate professionals grow with confidence, connection, and ease.

MORE BOOKS in the Mini Mastery Series

If you enjoyed this guide, you'll love all of Donna's handbooks for real estate professionals. Each book is concise, practical, and designed to give you great resources you can use right away. Scan this QR code to explore all of her books on Amazon. *And she's still creating more!*

www.ingramcontent.com/pod-product-compliance
Lightning Source LLC
Chambersburg PA
CBHW071146090426
42736CB00012B/2247